THIS LOG BELONGS TO

DATE/TIME	OIL CHANGED	AIR FILTER	ROTATE/ BALANCE TIRES	TIRE REPLACED	WHEEL ALIGNMENT	FUEL FILTER	BRAKES SERVICED	SPARK PLUGS	TRANSMISSION	WIPER BLADES	BATTERIES	RADIATOR	BELTS & HOSES	MILEAGE

OTHER MAINTENANCE

DATE/TIME	DESCRIPTION	MILEAGE

DATE/TIME	OIL CHANGED	AIR FILTER	ROTATE/ BALANCE TIRES	TIRE REPLACED	WHEEL ALIGNMENT	FUEL FILTER	BRAKES SERVICED	SPARK PLUGS	TRANSMISSION	WIPER BLADES	BATTERIES	RADIATOR	BELTS & HOSES	MILEAGE

OTHER MAINTENANCE

DATE/TIME	DESCRIPTION	MILEAGE

DATE/TIME	OIL CHANGED	AIR FILTER	ROTATE/ BALANCE TIRES	TIRE REPLACED	WHEEL ALIGNMENT	FUEL FILTER	BRAKES SERVICED	SPARK PLUGS	TRANSMISSION	WIPER BLADES	BATTERIES	RADIATOR	BELTS & HOSES	MILEAGE

OTHER MAINTENANCE

DATE/TIME	DESCRIPTION	MILEAGE

DATE/TIME	OIL CHANGED	AIR FILTER	ROTATE/ BALANCE TIRES	TIRE REPLACED	WHEEL ALIGNMENT	FUEL FILTER	BRAKES SERVICED	SPARK PLUGS	TRANSMISSION	WIPER BLADES	BATTERIES	RADIATOR	BELTS & HOSES	MILEAGE

OTHER MAINTENANCE

DATE/TIME	DESCRIPTION	MILEAGE

DATE/TIME	OIL CHANGED	AIR FILTER	ROTATE/ BALANCE TIRES	TIRE REPLACED	WHEEL ALIGNMENT	FUEL FILTER	BRAKES SERVICED	SPARK PLUGS	TRANSMISSION	WIPER BLADES	BATTERIES	RADIATOR	BELTS & HOSES	MILEAGE

OTHER MAINTENANCE

DATE/TIME	DESCRIPTION	MILEAGE

DATE/TIME	OIL CHANGED	AIR FILTER	ROTATE/ BALANCE TIRES	TIRE REPLACED	WHEEL ALIGNMENT	FUEL FILTER	BRAKES SERVICED	SPARK PLUGS	TRANSMISSION	WIPER BLADES	BATTERIES	RADIATOR	BELTS & HOSES	MILEAGE

OTHER MAINTENANCE

DATE/TIME	DESCRIPTION	MILEAGE

DATE/TIME	OIL CHANGED	AIR FILTER	ROTATE/ BALANCE TIRES	TIRE REPLACED	WHEEL ALIGNMENT	FUEL FILTER	BRAKES SERVICED	SPARK PLUGS	TRANSMISSION	WIPER BLADES	BATTERIES	RADIATOR	BELTS & HOSES	MILEAGE

OTHER MAINTENANCE

DATE/TIME	DESCRIPTION	MILEAGE

DATE/TIME	OIL CHANGED	AIR FILTER	ROTATE/ BALANCE TIRES	TIRE REPLACED	WHEEL ALIGNMENT	FUEL FILTER	BRAKES SERVICED	SPARK PLUGS	TRANSMISSION	WIPER BLADES	BATTERIES	RADIATOR	BELTS & HOSES	MILEAGE

OTHER MAINTENANCE

DATE/TIME	DESCRIPTION	MILEAGE

DATE/TIME	OIL CHANGED	AIR FILTER	ROTATE/ BALANCE TIRES	TIRE REPLACED	WHEEL ALIGNMENT	FUEL FILTER	BRAKES SERVICED	SPARK PLUGS	TRANSMISSION	WIPER BLADES	BATTERIES	RADIATOR	BELTS & HOSES	MILEAGE

OTHER MAINTENANCE

DATE/TIME	DESCRIPTION	MILEAGE

DATE/TIME	OIL CHANGED	AIR FILTER	ROTATE/ BALANCE TIRES	TIRE REPLACED	WHEEL ALIGNMENT	FUEL FILTER	BRAKES SERVICED	SPARK PLUGS	TRANSMISSION	WIPER BLADES	BATTERIES	RADIATOR	BELTS & HOSES	MILEAGE

OTHER MAINTENANCE

DATE/TIME	DESCRIPTION	MILEAGE

DATE/TIME	OIL CHANGED	AIR FILTER	ROTATE/ BALANCE TIRES	TIRE REPLACED	WHEEL ALIGNMENT	FUEL FILTER	BRAKES SERVICED	SPARK PLUGS	TRANSMISSION	WIPER BLADES	BATTERIES	RADIATOR	BELTS & HOSES	MILEAGE

OTHER MAINTENANCE

DATE/TIME	DESCRIPTION	MILEAGE

DATE/TIME	OIL CHANGED	AIR FILTER	ROTATE/ BALANCE TIRES	TIRE REPLACED	WHEEL ALIGNMENT	FUEL FILTER	BRAKES SERVICED	SPARK PLUGS	TRANSMISSION	WIPER BLADES	BATTERIES	RADIATOR	BELTS & HOSES	MILEAGE

OTHER MAINTENANCE

DATE/TIME	DESCRIPTION	MILEAGE

DATE/TIME	OIL CHANGED	AIR FILTER	ROTATE/ BALANCE TIRES	TIRE REPLACED	WHEEL ALIGNMENT	FUEL FILTER	BRAKES SERVICED	SPARK PLUGS	TRANSMISSION	WIPER BLADES	BATTERIES	RADIATOR	BELTS & HOSES	MILEAGE

OTHER MAINTENANCE

DATE/TIME	DESCRIPTION	MILEAGE

DATE/TIME	OIL CHANGED	AIR FILTER	ROTATE/ BALANCE TIRES	TIRE REPLACED	WHEEL ALIGNMENT	FUEL FILTER	BRAKES SERVICED	SPARK PLUGS	TRANSMISSION	WIPER BLADES	BATTERIES	RADIATOR	BELTS & HOSES	MILEAGE

OTHER MAINTENANCE

DATE/TIME	DESCRIPTION	MILEAGE

DATE/TIME	OIL CHANGED	AIR FILTER	ROTATE/ BALANCE TIRES	TIRE REPLACED	WHEEL ALIGNMENT	FUEL FILTER	BRAKES SERVICED	SPARK PLUGS	TRANSMISSION	WIPER BLADES	BATTERIES	RADIATOR	BELTS & HOSES	MILEAGE

OTHER MAINTENANCE

DATE/TIME	DESCRIPTION	MILEAGE

DATE/TIME	OIL CHANGED	AIR FILTER	ROTATE/ BALANCE TIRES	TIRE REPLACED	WHEEL ALIGNMENT	FUEL FILTER	BRAKES SERVICED	SPARK PLUGS	TRANSMISSION	WIPER BLADES	BATTERIES	RADIATOR	BELTS & HOSES	MILEAGE

OTHER MAINTENANCE

DATE/TIME	DESCRIPTION	MILEAGE

DATE/TIME	OIL CHANGED	AIR FILTER	ROTATE/ BALANCE TIRES	TIRE REPLACED	WHEEL ALIGNMENT	FUEL FILTER	BRAKES SERVICED	SPARK PLUGS	TRANSMISSION	WIPER BLADES	BATTERIES	RADIATOR	BELTS & HOSES	MILEAGE

OTHER MAINTENANCE

DATE/TIME	DESCRIPTION	MILEAGE

DATE/TIME	OIL CHANGED	AIR FILTER	ROTATE/ BALANCE TIRES	TIRE REPLACED	WHEEL ALIGNMENT	FUEL FILTER	BRAKES SERVICED	SPARK PLUGS	TRANSMISSION	WIPER BLADES	BATTERIES	RADIATOR	BELTS & HOSES	MILEAGE

OTHER MAINTENANCE

DATE/TIME	DESCRIPTION	MILEAGE

DATE/TIME	OIL CHANGED	AIR FILTER	ROTATE/ BALANCE TIRES	TIRE REPLACED	WHEEL ALIGNMENT	FUEL FILTER	BRAKES SERVICED	SPARK PLUGS	TRANSMISSION	WIPER BLADES	BATTERIES	RADIATOR	BELTS & HOSES	MILEAGE

OTHER MAINTENANCE

DATE/TIME	DESCRIPTION	MILEAGE

DATE/TIME	OIL CHANGED	AIR FILTER	ROTATE/ BALANCE TIRES	TIRE REPLACED	WHEEL ALIGNMENT	FUEL FILTER	BRAKES SERVICED	SPARK PLUGS	TRANSMISSION	WIPER BLADES	BATTERIES	RADIATOR	BELTS & HOSES	MILEAGE

OTHER MAINTENANCE

DATE/TIME	DESCRIPTION	MILEAGE

DATE/TIME	OIL CHANGED	AIR FILTER	ROTATE/ BALANCE TIRES	TIRE REPLACED	WHEEL ALIGNMENT	FUEL FILTER	BRAKES SERVICED	SPARK PLUGS	TRANSMISSION	WIPER BLADES	BATTERIES	RADIATOR	BELTS & HOSES	MILEAGE

OTHER MAINTENANCE

DATE/TIME	DESCRIPTION	MILEAGE

DATE/TIME	OIL CHANGED	AIR FILTER	ROTATE/ BALANCE TIRES	TIRE REPLACED	WHEEL ALIGNMENT	FUEL FILTER	BRAKES SERVICED	SPARK PLUGS	TRANSMISSION	WIPER BLADES	BATTERIES	RADIATOR	BELTS & HOSES	MILEAGE

OTHER MAINTENANCE

DATE/TIME	DESCRIPTION	MILEAGE

DATE/TIME	OIL CHANGED	AIR FILTER	ROTATE/ BALANCE TIRES	TIRE REPLACED	WHEEL ALIGNMENT	FUEL FILTER	BRAKES SERVICED	SPARK PLUGS	TRANSMISSION	WIPER BLADES	BATTERIES	RADIATOR	BELTS & HOSES	MILEAGE

OTHER MAINTENANCE

DATE/TIME	DESCRIPTION	MILEAGE

DATE/TIME	OIL CHANGED	AIR FILTER	ROTATE/ BALANCE TIRES	TIRE REPLACED	WHEEL ALIGNMENT	FUEL FILTER	BRAKES SERVICED	SPARK PLUGS	TRANSMISSION	WIPER BLADES	BATTERIES	RADIATOR	BELTS & HOSES	MILEAGE

OTHER MAINTENANCE

DATE/TIME	DESCRIPTION	MILEAGE

DATE/TIME	OIL CHANGED	AIR FILTER	ROTATE/ BALANCE TIRES	TIRE REPLACED	WHEEL ALIGNMENT	FUEL FILTER	BRAKES SERVICED	SPARK PLUGS	TRANSMISSION	WIPER BLADES	BATTERIES	RADIATOR	BELTS & HOSES	MILEAGE

OTHER MAINTENANCE

DATE/TIME	DESCRIPTION	MILEAGE

DATE/TIME	OIL CHANGED	AIR FILTER	ROTATE/ BALANCE TIRES	TIRE REPLACED	WHEEL ALIGNMENT	FUEL FILTER	BRAKES SERVICED	SPARK PLUGS	TRANSMISSION	WIPER BLADES	BATTERIES	RADIATOR	BELTS & HOSES	MILEAGE

OTHER MAINTENANCE

DATE/TIME	DESCRIPTION	MILEAGE

DATE/TIME	OIL CHANGED	AIR FILTER	ROTATE/ BALANCE TIRES	TIRE REPLACED	WHEEL ALIGNMENT	FUEL FILTER	BRAKES SERVICED	SPARK PLUGS	TRANSMISSION	WIPER BLADES	BATTERIES	RADIATOR	BELTS & HOSES	MILEAGE

OTHER MAINTENANCE

DATE/TIME	DESCRIPTION	MILEAGE

DATE/TIME	OIL CHANGED	AIR FILTER	ROTATE/ BALANCE TIRES	TIRE REPLACED	WHEEL ALIGNMENT	FUEL FILTER	BRAKES SERVICED	SPARK PLUGS	TRANSMISSION	WIPER BLADES	BATTERIES	RADIATOR	BELTS & HOSES	MILEAGE

OTHER MAINTENANCE

DATE/TIME	DESCRIPTION	MILEAGE

DATE/TIME	OIL CHANGED	AIR FILTER	ROTATE/ BALANCE TIRES	TIRE REPLACED	WHEEL ALIGNMENT	FUEL FILTER	BRAKES SERVICED	SPARK PLUGS	TRANSMISSION	WIPER BLADES	BATTERIES	RADIATOR	BELTS & HOSES	MILEAGE

OTHER MAINTENANCE

DATE/TIME	DESCRIPTION	MILEAGE

DATE/TIME	OIL CHANGED	AIR FILTER	ROTATE/ BALANCE TIRES	TIRE REPLACED	WHEEL ALIGNMENT	FUEL FILTER	BRAKES SERVICED	SPARK PLUGS	TRANSMISSION	WIPER BLADES	BATTERIES	RADIATOR	BELTS & HOSES	MILEAGE

OTHER MAINTENANCE

DATE/TIME	DESCRIPTION	MILEAGE

DATE/TIME	OIL CHANGED	AIR FILTER	ROTATE/ BALANCE TIRES	TIRE REPLACED	WHEEL ALIGNMENT	FUEL FILTER	BRAKES SERVICED	SPARK PLUGS	TRANSMISSION	WIPER BLADES	BATTERIES	RADIATOR	BELTS & HOSES	MILEAGE

OTHER MAINTENANCE

DATE/TIME	DESCRIPTION	MILEAGE

DATE/TIME	OIL CHANGED	AIR FILTER	ROTATE/ BALANCE TIRES	TIRE REPLACED	WHEEL ALIGNMENT	FUEL FILTER	BRAKES SERVICED	SPARK PLUGS	TRANSMISSION	WIPER BLADES	BATTERIES	RADIATOR	BELTS & HOSES	MILEAGE

OTHER MAINTENANCE

DATE/TIME	DESCRIPTION	MILEAGE

DATE/TIME	OIL CHANGED	AIR FILTER	ROTATE/ BALANCE TIRES	TIRE REPLACED	WHEEL ALIGNMENT	FUEL FILTER	BRAKES SERVICED	SPARK PLUGS	TRANSMISSION	WIPER BLADES	BATTERIES	RADIATOR	BELTS & HOSES	MILEAGE

OTHER MAINTENANCE

DATE/TIME	DESCRIPTION	MILEAGE

DATE/TIME	OIL CHANGED	AIR FILTER	ROTATE/ BALANCE TIRES	TIRE REPLACED	WHEEL ALIGNMENT	FUEL FILTER	BRAKES SERVICED	SPARK PLUGS	TRANSMISSION	WIPER BLADES	BATTERIES	RADIATOR	BELTS & HOSES	MILEAGE

OTHER MAINTENANCE

DATE/TIME	DESCRIPTION	MILEAGE

DATE/TIME	OIL CHANGED	AIR FILTER	ROTATE/ BALANCE TIRES	TIRE REPLACED	WHEEL ALIGNMENT	FUEL FILTER	BRAKES SERVICED	SPARK PLUGS	TRANSMISSION	WIPER BLADES	BATTERIES	RADIATOR	BELTS & HOSES	MILEAGE

OTHER MAINTENANCE

DATE/TIME	DESCRIPTION	MILEAGE

DATE/TIME	OIL CHANGED	AIR FILTER	ROTATE/ BALANCE TIRES	TIRE REPLACED	WHEEL ALIGNMENT	FUEL FILTER	BRAKES SERVICED	SPARK PLUGS	TRANSMISSION	WIPER BLADES	BATTERIES	RADIATOR	BELTS & HOSES	MILEAGE

OTHER MAINTENANCE

DATE/TIME	DESCRIPTION	MILEAGE

DATE/TIME	OIL CHANGED	AIR FILTER	ROTATE/ BALANCE TIRES	TIRE REPLACED	WHEEL ALIGNMENT	FUEL FILTER	BRAKES SERVICED	SPARK PLUGS	TRANSMISSION	WIPER BLADES	BATTERIES	RADIATOR	BELTS & HOSES	MILEAGE

OTHER MAINTENANCE

DATE/TIME	DESCRIPTION	MILEAGE

DATE/TIME	OIL CHANGED	AIR FILTER	ROTATE/ BALANCE TIRES	TIRE REPLACED	WHEEL ALIGNMENT	FUEL FILTER	BRAKES SERVICED	SPARK PLUGS	TRANSMISSION	WIPER BLADES	BATTERIES	RADIATOR	BELTS & HOSES	MILEAGE

OTHER MAINTENANCE

DATE/TIME	DESCRIPTION	MILEAGE

DATE/TIME	OIL CHANGED	AIR FILTER	ROTATE/ BALANCE TIRES	TIRE REPLACED	WHEEL ALIGNMENT	FUEL FILTER	BRAKES SERVICED	SPARK PLUGS	TRANSMISSION	WIPER BLADES	BATTERIES	RADIATOR	BELTS & HOSES	MILEAGE

OTHER MAINTENANCE

DATE/TIME	DESCRIPTION	MILEAGE

DATE/TIME	OIL CHANGED	AIR FILTER	ROTATE/ BALANCE TIRES	TIRE REPLACED	WHEEL ALIGNMENT	FUEL FILTER	BRAKES SERVICED	SPARK PLUGS	TRANSMISSION	WIPER BLADES	BATTERIES	RADIATOR	BELTS & HOSES	MILEAGE

OTHER MAINTENANCE

DATE/TIME	DESCRIPTION	MILEAGE

DATE/TIME	OIL CHANGED	AIR FILTER	ROTATE/ BALANCE TIRES	TIRE REPLACED	WHEEL ALIGNMENT	FUEL FILTER	BRAKES SERVICED	SPARK PLUGS	TRANSMISSION	WIPER BLADES	BATTERIES	RADIATOR	BELTS & HOSES	MILEAGE

OTHER MAINTENANCE

DATE/TIME	DESCRIPTION	MILEAGE

DATE/TIME	OIL CHANGED	AIR FILTER	ROTATE/ BALANCE TIRES	TIRE REPLACED	WHEEL ALIGNMENT	FUEL FILTER	BRAKES SERVICED	SPARK PLUGS	TRANSMISSION	WIPER BLADES	BATTERIES	RADIATOR	BELTS & HOSES	MILEAGE

OTHER MAINTENANCE

DATE/TIME	DESCRIPTION	MILEAGE

DATE/TIME	OIL CHANGED	AIR FILTER	ROTATE/ BALANCE TIRES	TIRE REPLACED	WHEEL ALIGNMENT	FUEL FILTER	BRAKES SERVICED	SPARK PLUGS	TRANSMISSION	WIPER BLADES	BATTERIES	RADIATOR	BELTS & HOSES	MILEAGE

OTHER MAINTENANCE

DATE/TIME	DESCRIPTION	MILEAGE

DATE/TIME	OIL CHANGED	AIR FILTER	ROTATE/ BALANCE TIRES	TIRE REPLACED	WHEEL ALIGNMENT	FUEL FILTER	BRAKES SERVICED	SPARK PLUGS	TRANSMISSION	WIPER BLADES	BATTERIES	RADIATOR	BELTS & HOSES	MILEAGE

OTHER MAINTENANCE

DATE/TIME	DESCRIPTION	MILEAGE

DATE/TIME	OIL CHANGED	AIR FILTER	ROTATE/ BALANCE TIRES	TIRE REPLACED	WHEEL ALIGNMENT	FUEL FILTER	BRAKES SERVICED	SPARK PLUGS	TRANSMISSION	WIPER BLADES	BATTERIES	RADIATOR	BELTS & HOSES	MILEAGE

OTHER MAINTENANCE

DATE/TIME	DESCRIPTION	MILEAGE

DATE/TIME	OIL CHANGED	AIR FILTER	ROTATE/ BALANCE TIRES	TIRE REPLACED	WHEEL ALIGNMENT	FUEL FILTER	BRAKES SERVICED	SPARK PLUGS	TRANSMISSION	WIPER BLADES	BATTERIES	RADIATOR	BELTS & HOSES	MILEAGE

OTHER MAINTENANCE

DATE/TIME	DESCRIPTION	MILEAGE

DATE/TIME	OIL CHANGED	AIR FILTER	ROTATE/ BALANCE TIRES	TIRE REPLACED	WHEEL ALIGNMENT	FUEL FILTER	BRAKES SERVICED	SPARK PLUGS	TRANSMISSION	WIPER BLADES	BATTERIES	RADIATOR	BELTS & HOSES	MILEAGE

OTHER MAINTENANCE

DATE/TIME	DESCRIPTION	MILEAGE

DATE/TIME	OIL CHANGED	AIR FILTER	ROTATE/ BALANCE TIRES	TIRE REPLACED	WHEEL ALIGNMENT	FUEL FILTER	BRAKES SERVICED	SPARK PLUGS	TRANSMISSION	WIPER BLADES	BATTERIES	RADIATOR	BELTS & HOSES	MILEAGE

OTHER MAINTENANCE

DATE/TIME	DESCRIPTION	MILEAGE

DATE/TIME	OIL CHANGED	AIR FILTER	ROTATE/ BALANCE TIRES	TIRE REPLACED	WHEEL ALIGNMENT	FUEL FILTER	BRAKES SERVICED	SPARK PLUGS	TRANSMISSION	WIPER BLADES	BATTERIES	RADIATOR	BELTS & HOSES	MILEAGE

OTHER MAINTENANCE

DATE/TIME	DESCRIPTION	MILEAGE

DATE/TIME	OIL CHANGED	AIR FILTER	ROTATE/ BALANCE TIRES	TIRE REPLACED	WHEEL ALIGNMENT	FUEL FILTER	BRAKES SERVICED	SPARK PLUGS	TRANSMISSION	WIPER BLADES	BATTERIES	RADIATOR	BELTS & HOSES	MILEAGE

OTHER MAINTENANCE

DATE/TIME	DESCRIPTION	MILEAGE

DATE/TIME	OIL CHANGED	AIR FILTER	ROTATE/ BALANCE TIRES	TIRE REPLACED	WHEEL ALIGNMENT	FUEL FILTER	BRAKES SERVICED	SPARK PLUGS	TRANSMISSION	WIPER BLADES	BATTERIES	RADIATOR	BELTS & HOSES	MILEAGE

OTHER MAINTENANCE

DATE/TIME	DESCRIPTION	MILEAGE

DATE/TIME	OIL CHANGED	AIR FILTER	ROTATE/ BALANCE TIRES	TIRE REPLACED	WHEEL ALIGNMENT	FUEL FILTER	BRAKES SERVICED	SPARK PLUGS	TRANSMISSION	WIPER BLADES	BATTERIES	RADIATOR	BELTS & HOSES	MILEAGE

OTHER MAINTENANCE

DATE/TIME	DESCRIPTION	MILEAGE

DATE/TIME	OIL CHANGED	AIR FILTER	ROTATE/ BALANCE TIRES	TIRE REPLACED	WHEEL ALIGNMENT	FUEL FILTER	BRAKES SERVICED	SPARK PLUGS	TRANSMISSION	WIPER BLADES	BATTERIES	RADIATOR	BELTS & HOSES	MILEAGE

OTHER MAINTENANCE

DATE/TIME	DESCRIPTION	MILEAGE

DATE/TIME	OIL CHANGED	AIR FILTER	ROTATE/ BALANCE TIRES	TIRE REPLACED	WHEEL ALIGNMENT	FUEL FILTER	BRAKES SERVICED	SPARK PLUGS	TRANSMISSION	WIPER BLADES	BATTERIES	RADIATOR	BELTS & HOSES	MILEAGE

OTHER MAINTENANCE

DATE/TIME	DESCRIPTION	MILEAGE

Made in the USA
Coppell, TX
18 March 2021

51965934R00066